PENGUIN BOOKS

BUTTERFLY MAGIC

An enduring interest in lepidopterology, begun in his native Norway, led Kjell B. Sandved to discover the vast collection of specimens in the National Museum of Natural History at the Smithsonian Institution, Washington, D.C. He soon began to study and photograph butterflies—in display cases, under microscopes, and eventually outdoors, stalking them for hours near river banks and along jungle paths. Today his files include photographs of thousands of species from all over the world. Now a producer of motion pictures on natural history for the Smithsonian, he uses "scenomacro" apparatus and special light-filtration systems that he himself devised. He was recently selected by the National Science Foundation to film the life of the Adélie penguins and their predators in Antarctica. *Natural History, National Wildlife,* and *Smithsonian* magazines, among others, frequently print the colorful results of his photographic investigations, and his third book, *Shells in Color,* with a text by R. Tucker Abbott, presents his loveliest studies of shells.

Born and educated in England, Michael G. Emsley has been a faculty member of the Department of Zoology at the University of the West Indies in Trinidad; resident director of the William Beebe Tropical Research Station, Trinidad; and Chairman of the Department of Entomology at the Academy of Natural Sciences in Philadelphia. He is currently Professor of Biology at George Mason University in Fairfax, Virginia, and editor of *Biotropica* (Journal of the Association for Tropical Biology Inc.).

BUTTERFLY MAGIC

Photographs by Kjell B. Sandved

Text by Michael G. Emsley

PENGUIN BOOKS

To the memory of William Beebe, naturalist and gentleman, whose writings have enriched the lives of many men and women all over the world.

Penguin Books Ltd, Harmondsworth, Middlesex, England
Penguin Books, 625 Madison Avenue, New York, New York 10022, U.S.A.
Penguin Books Australia Ltd, Ringwood, Victoria, Australia
Penguin Books Canada Ltd, 41 Steelcase Road West, Markham, Ontario, Canada
Penguin Books (N.Z.) Ltd, 182–190 Wairau Road, Auckland 10, New Zealand

First published in the United States of America by The Viking Press 1975
First published in Great Britain by Michael Joseph, Ltd., 1975
Published in Penguin Books 1976

LIBRARY OF CONGRESS CATALOGING IN PUBLICATION DATA
Sandved, Kjell Bloch, 1922—
Butterfly magic.
Bibliography: p.
1. Butterflies—Pictorial works. I. Emsley, Michael G. II. Title.
[QL543.S19 1976]   595.7'89   76–18684
ISBN 0 14 00.4289 X (pbk.)

Text printed in the United States of America by
Halliday Lithograph Corporation, West Hanover, Massachusetts
Set in Helvetica
Color photographs printed in Japan

We are grateful to Little, Brown & Co. and J. M. Dent & Sons, Ltd, for permission to use "The Purist" by Ogden Nash. Copyright 1935 by The Curtis Publishing Company, copyright renewed © Ogden Nash, 1963.

Contents

Foreword

The magic of butterflies. Can it be defined? Is it their flashes of color, their flittering flights, or the ease with which they defy you when you try to catch or photograph them? Or is it their scale formations, seen under the microscope as veritable fireworks of intense structural coloration, intermingled in a never-ending variety of patterns pigmented with soft pastel shades?

"The beauty of a butterfly's wing," writes Donald Culross Peattie in *An Almanac for Moderns,* "the beauty of all things, is not slave to purpose, a drudge sold to futurity. It is excrescence, superabundance, random ebullience, and sheer delightful waste to be enjoyed in its own high right."

As soon as the caterpillar puts on its gay wedding clothes, the fragile little creature fritters away its short existence in search of a mate—and its time is short, most of them living for a few days or a few weeks unseen by the eyes of man. This wealth and exquisite variety showered upon us by the Almighty is awesome. This richness of life makes us wonder. It makes us grateful.

When I first started looking through collections of butterflies fifteen years ago, I quickly became infatuated with the beautiful and variable designs in butterflies' wings. Not knowing how to photograph, I learned the hard way: by taking thousands upon thousands of closeup pictures in the Smithsonian

Institution's National Museum of Natural History. Most were bad, but they slowly got better. I managed to steer my photographic mania toward studying and photographing butterflies in the field. Eventually this took on a more meaningful direction and matured into the production of motion pictures documenting the behavior and life cycles of butterflies, as well as other life forms, for the scientific community.

While examining thousands of specimens under the microscope, I discovered that the wing patterns of tropical moths are just as attractive as those of butterflies. The differences between the color design in butterflies and in their night-flying cousins, the moths, are interesting. For one thing, I generally found most of the fascinating patterns in butterflies on the underside of their hindwings; in moths I found the most interesting color patterns on the upper side of their front wings. The reason for this is that butterflies normally rest with their wings folded vertically over their backs, whereas moths rest with their wings folded horizontally over their bodies. The design on their wings thus becomes a camouflage in evolutionary response to predation pressure.

Another difference between the designs is that in butterflies the patterns consistently have a more geometric or repetitive arrangement, whereas in moths the designs are much more variable and abstract (they remind me of carpets). The colors in butterflies are more vivid and structural than those of the moths, which tend to be pastel-pigmented shades. In looking at the marvelous kaleidoscopic designs of more than a million specimens, I have found the entire alphabet as well as the arabic numerals through 9.

On my numerous trips to various tropical countries around the world, I have spent many happy hours on butterfly safaris, shooting with my macro- and telephoto lenses. My favorite places for photographing tropical butterflies are near riverbanks or streams, or along jungle paths or glens. I have my best luck photographing them between eight and twelve in the morning when they are feeding on flowers. After noon they seem to prefer cooler hiding places in the shade. How exhilarating it is to stalk butterflies, even when crawl-ing slowly on all fours, as I did in the hot sun at the edge of a little trickling stream in a valley in New Guinea. The hours go by swiftly, and the cramps in the muscles mount, but the close observation enables me to get photographs of butterflies I have never seen before.

How rewarding after such a hot tropical day to walk home to my little abode and slake my thirst after a machete chop into a coconut! Or, as I once did in the Galápagos Islands, taste the delicious fruit of the *Opuntia echios* (cactus flower) and then spend the next hour trying to pick out the fine spines from my fingers!

Butterfly Magic offers only a glimpse into the fascinating world of butter-flies, but I hope it will make the reader more aware that the world of living things around us always has something new to give—if only we are receptive.

I am very grateful to The Viking Press for publishing my photographs and to Dr. Michael G. Emsley for writing the instructive text. I extend my gratitude to the National Museum of Natural History, the Smithsonian Institution, for permission to photograph certain specimens in their incomparable collection. My sincere thanks to all my friends at the Smithsonian Institution for early encouragement fifteen years ago when this work was only being planned. A special thanks to all my field assistants and friends in many countries for their help in making this book a reality. I am particularly grateful to the following persons: Donald M. Anderson, Edward S. Ayensu, Barbara A. Bedette, James P. Cramer, W. Donald Duckworth, Douglas C. Ferguson, William D. Field, Richard C. Froeschner, Robert D. Gordon, Francis M. Greenwell, Porter M. Kier, Lloyd V. Knutson, Curtis W. Sabrosky, Thomas R. Soderstrom, Rose Ella Warner Spilman, Ted J. Spilman, George C. Steyskal, Edward L. Todd, all of the Smithsonian Institution; Graziela M. Barros, Jardim Botanico do Rio de Janeiro; Clifford O. Berg, Cornell University; William M. Briggs, Victoria University of Wellington, New Zealand; Charles E. Cutress, University of Puerto Rico; Robert L. Dressler and Amada A. Reimer, Smithsonian Tropical Research Institute, Canal Zone; Howard E. Evans, University of Colorado; Graham Bell Fairchild, Panama City; Italo Claudio Falesi, IPEAN, Belém, Brazil; M. P. Harris, the Galápagos Islands; Kenneth P. Lamb, University of Papua and New Guinea; Martin Naumann, University of Connecticut; Ivan Polunin, University of Singapore; Diomedes Quintero, Universidad de Panama; Margot Schumm, Montgomery Community College, Virginia; Laura Schuster, Universidad A. de la Selva, Peru; Roman Vishniac, Yeshiva University; Thomas J. Walker, University of Florida; Dave Wapinsky, University of Virginia; Kirsten Wegener-Kofoed; and Fernández Yépez, University of Maracay, Venezuela.

Kjell B. Sandved
Smithsonian Institution
Washington, D.C.

Writing this book has been exciting, for it has caused me to reflect on my life at Simla, the tropical field station of the New York Zoological Society, in Trinidad. I shall always be in debt to the scientists and other visitors who came to Simla, for the wealth of experience and infectious enthusiasm they brought with them. I profited greatly, and I am very sad that the station is now closed. Some of my friends and colleagues are identified in this book, and to them in particular I express my thanks for the substantial contribution they made to my understanding of biology.

I am grateful to Little, Brown and Company, Curtis Brown, Ltd., and J. M. Dent & Sons Ltd. for their permission to publish "The Purist," and, of course, to my wife, Janet, for her continued patience and understanding.

Michael G. Emsley
George Mason University
Fairfax, Virginia

Butterfly Magic? 1

I give you now Professor Twist,
A conscientious scientist.
Trustees exclaimed, "He never bungles!"
And sent him off to distant jungles.

Camped on a tropic riverside,
One day he missed his loving bride.
She had, the guide informed him later,
Been eaten by an alligator.
Professor Twist could not but smile.
"You mean," he said, "a crocodile."

Ogden Nash. "The Purist," from *Family Reunion*

Professor Twist could never have agreed to the use of the word "magic" in the title of a book on butterflies. He would never have accepted that their senses and sensualities were the "products of sorcery or the occult powers of nature." But, not being purists and being tinged with more than a touch of romance, we can be persuaded that butterflies "produce effects by super-human means." Man cannot manufacture butterflies, so "magic" may be the appropriate word, not perhaps just for their sometimes flamboyant, sometimes subtle displays of color, but for the extraordinary complexity of their activities and perceptions. Magic it is that in a brain the size of a pinhead there are timers, stimulators, regulators, inhibitors, and co-ordinators of lives that are rich in maternal preparation, compulsive lust, visual deception, and gourmet delight.

We do not know how a butterfly works. We do not know how an egg becomes first a caterpillar, then a chrysalis, and then a butterfly—only that it does. Now and then we gain a little insight, but no more than you would of a hotel kitchen by looking in the doorway as the waiters pass in and out. At our present level of knowledge these developmental and behavioral processes may as well be magic, and therein lies the source of mystery, challenge, and excitement that forms the basis of this book.

The Butterfly Time Clock II

Nearly twenty years ago Jocelyn Crane Griffin, working at the William Beebe Tropical Research Station in Trinidad, asked herself, "How does a male butterfly recognize his own female when there are so many other species with which one species can be confused?"

Because of the simplicity of its color pattern, Jocelyn chose to study *Heliconius erato,* whose jet-black upper side is interrupted only by an oval patch of red on each forewing. In Trinidad the butterfly is known locally as the Postman because its colors match the uniform of the Trinidadian mailmen.

Color seemed the most likely candidate for the species recognition signal, for nearly all butterflies are brightly colored and fly at a time when colors can be most easily distinguished. The first step was to obtain an optical evaluation of the colors of the Postman, for the human eye can be deceived. We are unable, for instance, to see light of shorter wavelength than that of the violet end of the spectrum, whereas the eyes of many species of insects are known to be highly sensitive to these rays. Only when armed with detailed knowledge is it possible to match the colors of the butterfly with paints that not only look similar to us but that really are exact copies.

In 1942 Niko Tinbergen and his co-workers at Oxford had shown that the male Grayling butterfly was attracted to any dark fluttering object, regardless of color. Shape was important but motion was essential. The Grayling is a mottled tawny brown so we should not be surprised to find that color plays only a small part in its search for a mate. With Tinbergen's experiments as a base, Jocelyn teased Postmen in the insectary with lures of various colors and materials, each attached by a magnet to the end of a whippy stick. Again, motion proved essential, but a paper model butterfly with wings painted to match exactly the red of the Postman's wings was the most attractive decoy. Lures of other colors were quite ineffective.

As in any scientific investigation, each answer only leads to another question. In this case, "Does the butterfly learn that its mate is red, or does the butterfly emerge from the chrysalis with this information?" Finding out proved relatively simple. Jocelyn raised adults in a lightproof box and painted out their red wing markings with black enamel before they were able to see their own wings. When introduced to other Postmen in the insectary, they recognized their mates immediately; clearly, they had become adult already equipped with the knowledge that their mates were red.

Does the Postman see all colors or only red? Some of the best experiments are also the simplest. The use of sophisticated apparatus can sometimes become an end in itself, and the original objective becomes lost in the enthusiasm for the instruments. Tropical investigators are less prone to fall into this trap for they habitually work on shoestring budgets which reward only innovation and ingenuity. Jocelyn placed Postmen in a box into which light was admitted only through a small window at the top. At times during which the butterflies would normally be active the window was covered with a succession of glass filters, each of which admitted only a narrow range of colored light of known wavelength. If the butterflies in the box fluttered up to the window, they were deemed trying to escape and must have been able to see the light for which that particular filter was transparent. The results of

16

this simple experiment indicated that the butterflies could see all the spectral colors from red to the ultraviolet. This was an important discovery, for it meant that the butterflies were reacting to red not because it was the only color that they could see, but because red was being specially selected as significant out of the full range of colors. This tentative result demanded more sophisticated investigation.

During the early 1960s money flowing from the National Science Foundation of the United States of America and other funding agencies supported many researchers who visited the Trinidad field station. Among them was Stewart Swihart who was already interested in the color vision of insects and who readily agreed to collaborate in the studies on *Heliconius erato.* A skilled neurophysiologist, Stewart soon had an *erato* pinned out on the laboratory table with an electrode in one of the optic nerves that connects the eye to the brain. By serially focusing colored light of known wavelength and intensity onto the captive eye, and recording the electrical activity in the optic nerve with an oscilloscope (which works like a television tube), it was possible to confirm that the butterfly eye did indeed register all colors from red to ultraviolet. However, it is still debatable whether the insect sees colors as we understand them. Even when all precautions are taken, it is impossible to say what the animal sees, only that it sees some distinction in colors.

A repeat of the experiment with the electrodes in the brain produced a different result. Greater responses were obtained with red light than with any other color, except in the early morning, when yellow seemed more important. This result led to the final and most original experiment in this series.

Stewart had sometime previously acquired a long length of very fine insulated wire made of nichrome steel, which is immensely strong. It was the possession of this wire that gave him an exciting idea. He embedded a pair of electrodes in the brain of a free-flying but caged Postman and attached many feet of the wire, which was as thin as the thread of a spider's web, from the electrodes to an oscilloscope. With this setup he monitored the electrical activity of the brain of the insect under out-of-doors conditions for the several days that the butterfly lived in the insectary. During the night the Postman "slept" for the brain emitted only background noise signals that were consistent with a resting situation. However, with the arrival of dawn the level of nervous activity accelerated. Moving objects were found to be stimulating, particularly those that were yellow. Red appeared no more exciting than other colors. But at 8:30 a.m. a transformation took place—as if by magic. No longer was yellow of interest—only red. Somewhere in the butterfly's body a switch had been thrown which unleashed the response to red as a sexual signal, and the butterfly was then obliged to explore and court. By nine o'clock the response to red was at its peak and courtship was most intense, but throughout the remainder of the day it declined so that by four o'clock in the afternoon interest had almost entirely gone.

What controls the switch? Could it be environmental cues, such as the increasing light intensity or temperature as the morning sun rises? To investigate this, Stewart kept butterflies in the dark for three or four days and then tested them in the laboratory where the light and temperature conditions were quite different from those in the insectary. The switch was still there at the same time as usual, so it had to be governed by an internal rhythm working independently of outside conditions.

There are two lessons for us here. First, consider the superb degree of adaptation illustrated by this situation. The butterfly, male or female, is programmed to seek food from flowers of any hue, but most earnestly from those of the commonest color among native South American flowers, namely yellow. It is aided in the search by its attraction to movement, such as that of flowers being gently blown by the morning breeze. It is prevented from being distracted into early-morning courtship by the switching-off of the red-orientated courtship-releasing mechanism. It is as if the butterfly were not allowed to

18

turn to matters sexual until after it had had a hearty breakfast. Then, at 8:30 a.m. the serious work of the day can begin! Magic? Perhaps not, but surely marvelous.

The second lesson is that we consistently underestimate the complexity of organisms other than ourselves. Investigators continue to test only limited selections of insects—say a grasshopper, a beetle, and a butterfly—and from these limited sources of information they proceed to make sweeping generalizations about insects as a whole. We see here that not only does a butterfly have its own individuality as a species, but it may even behave differently at different times of the day.

We have little conception of the true complexity of even the most common insects. Consider that when next you swat a fly!

Butterfly Mating III

In all the experiments with paper models, the interest of the male butterflies quickly faded after the initial interception, suggesting that some factor possessed by virgin females was lacking. Experienced collectors can distinguish between mated and unmated female butterflies by their odor, but it is the mated, not the unmated, females which have the detectable scent; in the case of the Postman the odor has been likened to that of witch hazel. Ironically, the few investigations that have been conducted on the odors of butterflies have shown that the components that we can smell have no effect on other butterflies. It is the substances that we cannot smell that are the active ingredients. However, we are still ignorant of the features by which a virgin female is recognized.

The Postman awakes shortly after sunrise, which in most tropical latitudes is within half an hour of six o'clock. Due to the evaporation of water from the tree canopy and the protection of the forest floor from direct sunlight during the day, the night temperatures in tropical forests frequently fall below 50 degrees Fahrenheit. Those butterflies which roost in grasslands do not experience such low temperatures, and they usually have little difficulty in abosrbing sufficient heat for flight, for to absorb heat rapidly they have only to present themselves broadside to the morning sun.

However, forest species like the Postman have to shiver their flight muscles to generate enough heat to raise their body temperature to an effective level. Some temperate butterflies have to be at 84 degrees Fahrenheit before they can fly. Once warm enough, the Postman flies off in search of food. Flowers of all colors are visited, except green ones, which are usually wind pollinated, though there is slight preference for yellow. In tropical America yellow is a very common color for insect-pollinated flowers, for most of the native red flowers are adapted for pollination by hummingbirds which have good color vision. Most bees, including the honeybee, which was introduced into America by the early settlers in the middle of the seventeenth century, are red-blind, so red is a relatively uncommon color outside of ornamental varieties bred by man.

When the 8:30 a.m. switch is thrown, the male and unmated female Postmen display themselves around such red or orange flowers as lantana (*Lantana camara*) and milkweed (*Asclepias curassavica*). All moving red objects are inspected, and if a virgin female enters the group she is courted vigorously by several males. The males compete by trying to catch up with the now-fleeing female, and only the most persistent and maneuverable aerial gymnast stays in the race. Once the less fit males have been left behind, a ritualized pattern of courtship begins. The male Postman overtakes the female from above, passing very closely and dropping down in front of her. The female then overtakes the male by passing above him, so the pair seem to be tumbling over each other repeatedly. It may be that male odors are disseminated during the chase, for the close proximity of the male when passing over the female would bring his hindwing scent scales very near to the sense organs on the antennae of the female. Cinematography supports the idea that some substance is discharged from the hindwings during this part of the chase. For the courtship to be successful the female must be urged to lower and lower altitudes until she settles on a fence post, tree trunk, or other reasonably open surface. With the male hovering overhead and oscillating to and fro, the female closes her wings and raises and exposes the tip of her abdomen. It is interesting to notice here that during the experiments conducted by Stewart Swihart, flickering colors were found to be much more effective than still exposures and the most stimulating flicker frequency of all was between 20 and 26 exposures per second. The wing beat frequency of a hovering courting male Postman is 26 beats per second.

After about half a minute of fanning from above, the male alights in front of the female and turns to face her. Their antennae are now close to each other, though not in contact. The male advances and passes to one side of the female, usually on her left side, and when his head is alongside the base of her wings, he stops, turns a full 180 degrees, as if the head were a pivot, and with his terminal pincerlike appendages he grips the tip of the abdomen of the female. Only in this position can the penis be introduced into the female genital duct. The subsequent inflation of the penis ensures that it penetrates into the blind-ending sac where the sperm have to be deposited. When the penis is securely in place, the male again moves around through a semicircle so he faces the opposite direction of the female. In this tail-to-tail position they usually remain motionless for several hours or even overnight, but if disturbed the male will take flight with the female hanging on behind as a passive payload.

When the sperm are deposited in the copulatory sac, they are packaged in a skinlike envelope, and as the penis is withdrawn, a gelatinous material is deposited in the genital duct which hardens to form a plug, presumably to prevent the sperm from draining out but perhaps to prevent a second copulation being successful. Mated females are rarely courted and seem reluctant to accept even the most persistent males, but multiple inseminations have been recorded even in the presence of a plug.

22

The female normally stores sufficient sperm from her one mating to fertilize all the 150 or so eggs she will lay during her lifetime. To ensure their longevity, the sperm are moved from the copulatory sac to another repository, where nurse cells in the wall of the chamber nourish the sperm and keep them healthy until they are needed.

To return to the courtship. On the underside of the base of the hindwings of *Heliconius erato,* and in fact on all of the nearly fifty other species of *Heliconius,* there are a number of small red spots. From the observance of many courtships it seemed likely that the male was using these markings as a point of reference to indicate the moment when he was in the correct position to turn around. We interrupted a mating just prior to the male grasping the posterior of the female (so we knew the individuals were normal) and painted out the red spots on the female. When the butterflies were allowed to court again, everything proceeded as before until the male was alongside the female in the position in which he should have stopped and turned around; sure enough, he did not stop, but kept on walking until he had left the puzzled female far behind. Similar results were obtained with other individuals, though once a male climbed the wing of the female and with his left eye applied closely to her red forewing patch he groped hopelessly and helplessly in the air. With hindsight, we should have painted the red spots back onto the base of the wing of a female and have tried to establish a successful courtship with man-made signals.

In all insect behavior experiments it becomes clear that the animals are programmed to respond only to a predetermined set of signals. If any signal is missing, the behavioral sequence must stop and cannot be restarted without going all the way back to the beginning. In the courtship routine there is no ability to adapt to new circumstances. If a cue is missing, the courtship stops.

Experiments such as these make one wonder if there are any truly irrelevant or unnecessary components of a butterfly's color pattern. Is our lack of understanding just an index of our ignorance? I suspect that it is.

While the male continues to philander, the fertilized females are engaged in the serious business of laying eggs. Several days elapse after mating, during which time the eggs are maturing and the sperm are transferred to their permanent location. When the oldest eggs are ready for laying the female's behavior changes, for, after the early-morning feed, green seems the preferred color. The females spend all their time inspecting the leaves of shrubs, weeds, and vines to see if they are suitable depositories for their eggs. This change in behavior takes them out of the pool of exhibitionists disporting themselves in the sun, and the gravid females are to be found only where the food plants of their caterpillars grow. In her search for the correct food, the female flies slowly, and painstakingly explores every leaf she encounters. The testing of the leaf entails touching it with her condensed front feet, which are modified terminally into a battery of club-shaped hairs. The sense organs embedded in the tips of the hairs recognize only the odor exuded by leaves of the right food plant, so it is a "go" or "no-go" system. If the food plant is uncommon the female may fly many miles in search of a plant which gives the "go" signal. However, even when the correct plant is found, the presence of an egg of another Postman on the tender growing point, which is the preferred site for egg-laying, will enforce the seeking of an unoccupied shoot. As the female lays only about two or three eggs each day she has plenty of time. Fortunately, the *Passiflora tuberosa* vine upon which the caterpillars feed is very common in newly cut forests so the females rarely have to travel far.

Adults of *Heliconius erato,* in common with some other members of *Heliconius,* are unusual in that they return to the same roost every evening. It is really quite exciting to sit down by a particular grass stem or vine at about

24

5:30 p.m. and wait for previously marked butterflies to return. One by one they fly in and lazily settle upside down on the same roost as the night before, sometimes even in the same position. One may find up to twenty or so individuals of several species, males and females, roosting together night after night. The roosting colonies tend to be composed of older butterflies, recognizable by their faded colors and tattered wings. From time to time individuals do not return as they fall victim to age or predation. Vacancies in the roost are taken by younger butterflies, so the roosting colony can persist for many months.

Population studies have shown that though the Postmen show no signs of territoriality, they never stray more than about half a mile from their roost. It seems likely that the area occupied by a colony is determined principally by the distribution of plants in flower during a particular season, so as flowering patterns change so does the location of the colony.

The extreme difference between the behavior of male and gravid female Postmen may be a clue to the gross inequities in the representation of females of many species in museum collections. In some cases females are unknown or are represented by only a few specimens, whereas males would seem to be abundant by comparison. The reason is probably that the collector finds a "good locality" where flowers are plentiful, and in the knowledge that most butterfly species are most active in the morning or early afternoon, he works the locality thoroughly. However, in the search for food plants for their caterpillars, the egg-laying females may be confined to the canopy of the trees or the shaded interior of the forest. With so many butterflies in the sunshine what collector dares to move away!

I once took Bernard Heineman, co-author with F. Martin Brown of *Jamaica and Its Butterflies,* to a "good locality" in Trinidad, and we felt very pleased to have captured nearly fifty species in the course of the day. However, Keith Brown has taken more than four hundred species from a "good locality'' in Brazil, but only by making a rigorous effort to catch the smallest and most unobtrusive species and by collecting continuously throughout all seasons. In our defense, I should point out that the complete faunal list of Trinidadian butterflies totals only a little over five hundred species, which is much less than that of Brazil, so to see 10 per cent on a single day is not all that bad.

Malcolm Barcant, who has collected butterflies in Trinidad ever since he was a boy some forty years ago, has a virtually complete collection of all recorded species, with the exception of the Skippers. He used his own specimens to illustrate his book on the island's butterfly fauna. During a trip we made together to Ecuador he collected well over two hundred species, and humbled me on many occasions with his demonstration of the superiority of wisdom over youth. Once, we collected Owl-butterflies (Brassolidae), which are sometimes called Six-o'clocks because it is at dusk that they fly. They are creatures of habit and promenade tantalizingly along the edges of streams and forest paths. Though I was proud of my athleticism, the butterflies showed me time after time that I could not sprint as fast as they could fly. Malcolm just hid in the shadow of a large tree and snatched them from the air with his net as they flew past. The secret of the successful collector or photographer is patience.

All the butterflies I have caught since I was a boy have been free. Free, that is, to me, in that I paid for their capture only in patience and muscular effort. But butterflies themselves are not free; they are captives of their own inheritance. They have no free will. Their response to any given circumstance can be accurately predicted by anyone who knows their behavior well.

To Survive! IV

Lincoln and Jane Brower performed an experiment a few years ago that helps us understand the protective devices used by butterflies to avoid being eaten. Monarch butterflies (*Danaus plexippus*) were reared in the laboratory, some of the caterpillars being fed with cabbage and others with milkweed, the wild food plant. A number of insect-eating birds were also reared from eggs to act as inexperienced test predators. When all the animals were ready, a naïve bird was offered a Monarch whose caterpillar had been raised on cabbage. It was accepted and eaten immediately. This test-feeding was repeated many times with different birds and the butterflies were all devoured. However, when a Monarch, which as a caterpillar had been raised on milkweed, was offered, though it was accepted in the same way as its predecessors, its swallowing was followed at once by vomiting and an appearance of gross discomfort. The bird retched repeatedly, shook its head, and wiped its beak on its perch and the walls of its cage. This test bird, and all the others which were later exposed to a similar experience, refused any Monarch thereafter, regardless of what the caterpillars had been fed. The birds learned from one bad experience that some of these butterflies were acutely distasteful and from then on rejected them all. The lesson was remembered for many months.

The distasteful properties of adult butterflies clearly come from the food plants eaten by them when they were caterpillars. The cardiac glycosides of the milkweed (*Asclepias curassavica*) are absorbed by the caterpillar without adverse effect, stored in the chrysalis, and then incorporated into the body of the adult butterfly. There is enough poison in one Monarch to kill a small- to medium-size bird if the insect is not expelled. By surviving the encounter, the bird remembers not to eat that particular kind of butterfly again. Ironically, the plant probably produced the poison initially to protect itself from being eaten by caterpillars! There are many poisonous plants, and some whole families are characteristically poisonous—for example, Asclepiadaceae, Aristolochiaceae, Passifloraceae, and Solanaceae. So all the caterpillars that have become able to tolerate the poisons have relatively little competition for food when compared with those that feed on generally edible plants. Distasteful butterflies tend to have very bright colors and are therefore easily recognized by predators. If all the distasteful butterflies in one locality looked alike, then the predators would have to learn only one pattern. The sacrifice of a single individual of any species with the common pattern would provide protection for all the others from that particular predator. Mimicry of this kind has arisen in many kinds of butterflies. The theory was first proposed by Fritz Müller in 1878 as an explanation for the many similar-looking butterflies he encountered along the banks of the Amazon.

However, Henry Bates had already put forward an alternative hypothesis in 1864, following his trip up the Amazon between 1849 and 1860. He too had noticed the large number of butterflies belonging to different families which looked remarkably similar. So similar in fact that he was unable to distinguish them in flight, and only with difficulty in the hand. He argued that if a distasteful butterfly species gains protection from its predators by their learning to recognize its color pattern and subsequently avoiding it, then any butterfly, even an edible one, which has that pattern will deceive the predator and so escape being eaten. We now know that there are many similar-looking butterflies which fly together, some of which are poisonous and some of which are not. Both Bates and Müller were right some of the time.

Students of evolution enjoy themselves enormously when discussing mimicry. You can, for instance, argue that the distasteful models must be more abundant than the tasty mimics or the odds are in favor of the birds eating nearly all the mimics before they encounter a distasteful model. On the other hand, if there are only a few acutely distasteful models, one experience of which might be remembered for a lifetime, then perhaps they could provide sufficient protection for a greater number of tasty mimics. All arguments are handicapped by our unfortunate lack of reliable knowledge of which species are actually poisonous and which are not. Even the results of experiments in which substantial numbers of butterflies have been offered to naïve birds are clouded by the realization that elsewhere, or at other seasons of the year, another food plant might be consumed by the caterpillars which could materially alter the adult's tastiness.

I am reminded of an event which took place in Trinidad some time ago but which I shall never forget. We had been discussing mimicry at great length, and I had suggested that we set up a tasting panel to find out which butterflies seemed likely to be protected and which did not. I readily agreed that any comparison between palatability to a man and to a bird should be treated cautiously, but I thought it would be interesting. On a day when we were out in the field someone came up to me with a butterfly in her hand. She was holding it so the abdomen was wiggling in the air like a finger. "All right," she said, "you have been doing a lot of talking. How about a little action? Eat this!" Never one to reject a challenge, I hastily bit into the abdomen and chewed on it. To my amazement and relief, it had no taste at all. It was as if I had eaten a piece of cooking fat wrapped in brown paper. "Bring me another," I exclaimed, fired up with my newfound prowess as an insect eater. This was a mistake; I should have stopped while I was ahead. The next insect was absolutely horrendous. The lining of my mouth and the surface of my tongue turned to sandpaper. All trace of saliva disappeared and my mouth was filled with a quinine-like bitterness which resisted all my attempts to wipe it away. I put on as brave a face as I could muster, but I was lost. I could not conceal my discomfort. "Have another!" they jeered, obviously feeling no sympathy, but my tasting days were over—forever. I now know how Brower's birds felt, and I feel for them.

Some of the mimetic relationships in butterflies are quite mind-boggling, and the early naturalists must be excused for their confusion. One of the now classic cases of mimicry is that of *Papilio dardanus,* an African swallowtail in which the males are all reasonably uniform and are swallow-tailed in shape, whereas the females present a wide variety of appearances, even from within a single brood. Some females look like males, others look quite unlike swallowtails at all. However, the female patterns can all be matched with the color patterns of butterflies that occur in the same locality and whose caterpillars feed on poisonous plants. In different localities the proportion of the various females varies with the abundance of the appropriate models. The *dardanus* situation is not an isolated one, though it is perhaps the most famous because of the genetical studies conducted in Liverpool, England, by Philip Sheppard and C. A. Clarke. They have shown, in a twenty-year series of greenhouse breeding experiments, that there are a series of genetic units, each of which is responsible for the visible characteristics of one type of female. The expression of this genetic unit is modified by the other genes with which it is associated, so there is considerable variation among individual butterflies carrying the same genetic unit. This variation is the raw material upon which selection acts. The least perfect mimics are weeded out by being eaten, while those which are a really close match survive, reproduce, and perpetuate the effective pattern.

30

Recent work by Keith Brown and Woodruff Benson in Brazil has explained yet another complex situation that has had collectors and biologists baffled for more than a hundred years. *Heliconius numata* presents a bewildering number of different color forms. As many as five or six substantially different color patterns may be bred from a single clutch of eggs. When one considers the range of the species as a whole, several dozen forms can be identified. All seem potentially capable of interbreeding and are clearly members of a single species. Why this diversity? The answer seems to be that though *numata* is mildly toxic to birds, it lives in close proximity to various members of the highly poisonous Ithomiidae. However, the problem is that the ithomine adults are available as models for only short periods during the year. One species may be on the wing for a month or so, only to be replaced by another, perhaps quite different-looking one. The *numata,* in contrast, are long-lived, breed continuously, and produce adults throughout the whole year, so no single pattern will succeed in all seasons. Sometimes one pattern will be successful, sometimes another, depending on the abundance of the various models available. So, rather than rely on a single pattern, they have specialized in diversity and have produced a number of forms so that at least one of them will be appropriate as the models emerge. One is reminded of the maxim that one should not put all one's eggs in one basket. If *numata* had a coat of arms, that surely would be its motto.

The theorists say that for mimicry to begin, there must be a mutation which changes the pattern of the non-mimetic edible butterfly sufficiently for there to be at least a slight resemblance to an inedible model. From that beginning the predator will select out all the poorest copies by eating them, so the remainder will breed more of the better ones. Gradually the selection process will become so refined that only the most exact copies will survive and we will find the mimicry "fantastic," "incredible," "magical."

But what about the edible species which have no resemblance to distasteful models? To have survived for us to observe them, they must have some device which affords them protection from their enemies. Some rely on speed and maneuverability; others have false eyes and antennae to draw attention away from vital parts; still others depend on the excellence of their camouflage once they have alighted. Many examples of these techniques are illustrated in the colored plates that follow.

In explaining how and why butterflies are the colors they are, one must never lose sight of the fact that their colors have to serve two purposes: that of species recognition for mate selection, and for escape from predators. Sometimes these functions will be in conflict with each other and the final result is a compromise, but we can be sure that the compromise is effective or the species would have already become extinct.

When I was younger I used to wonder why more butterflies were not green, for that seemed the perfect color for camouflage. But if butterflies were green, think of the time and energy they might waste courting the leaves of trees!

Though collecting butterflies is fun, the real fun is in unraveling the secrets of their success. The magician holds us spellbound, but how satisfying it is to work out how he performs his tricks. Butterflies have no magic; it is us who are as children, probing the mysteries of their evolution.

4

5

6

7

8

9

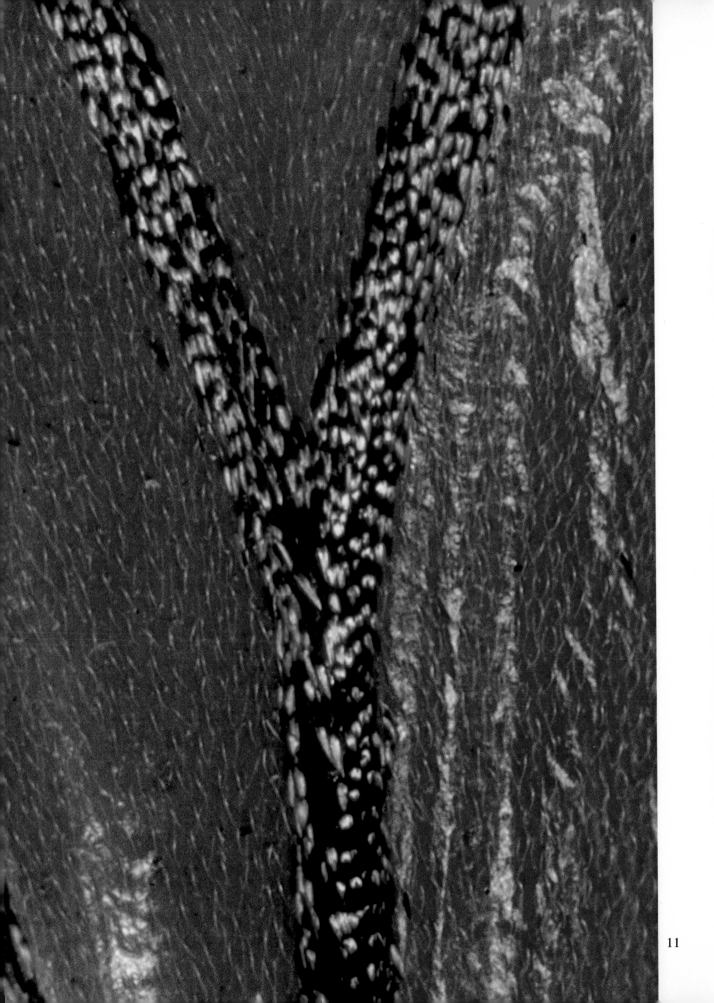

11

14

15

16

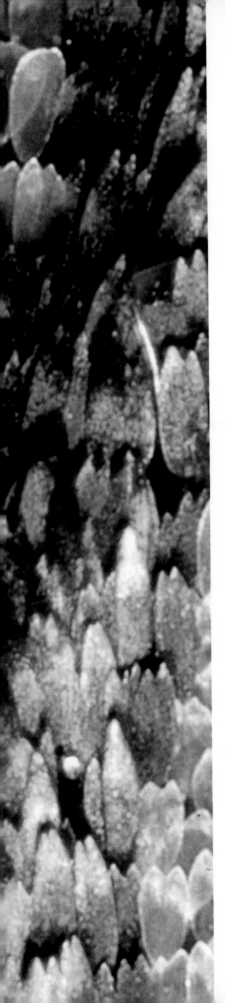

17

18

19

20

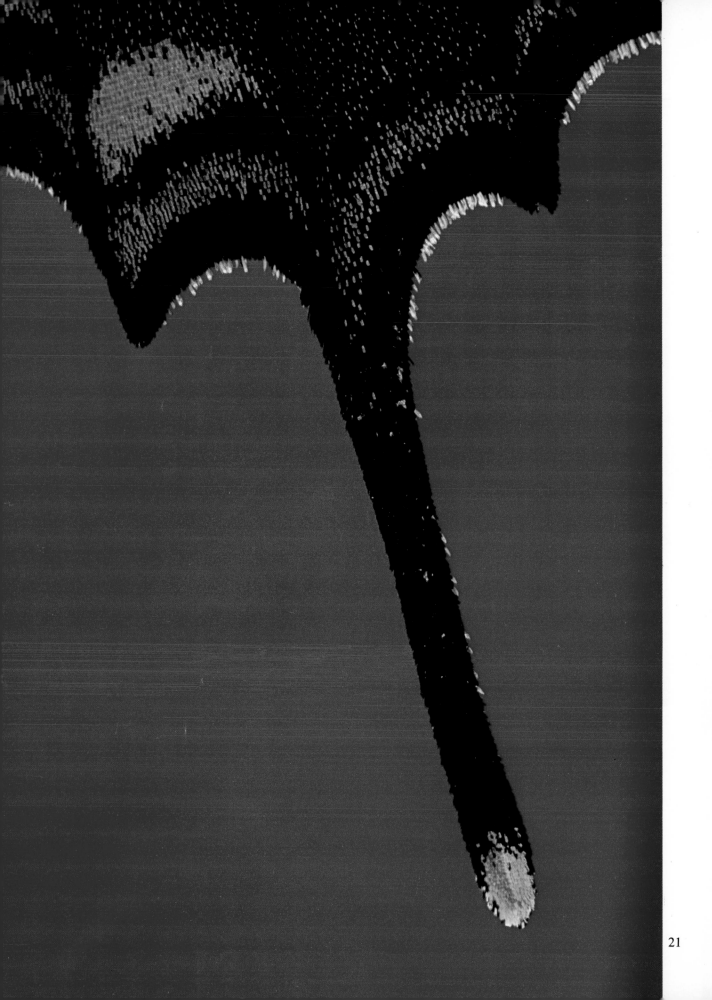

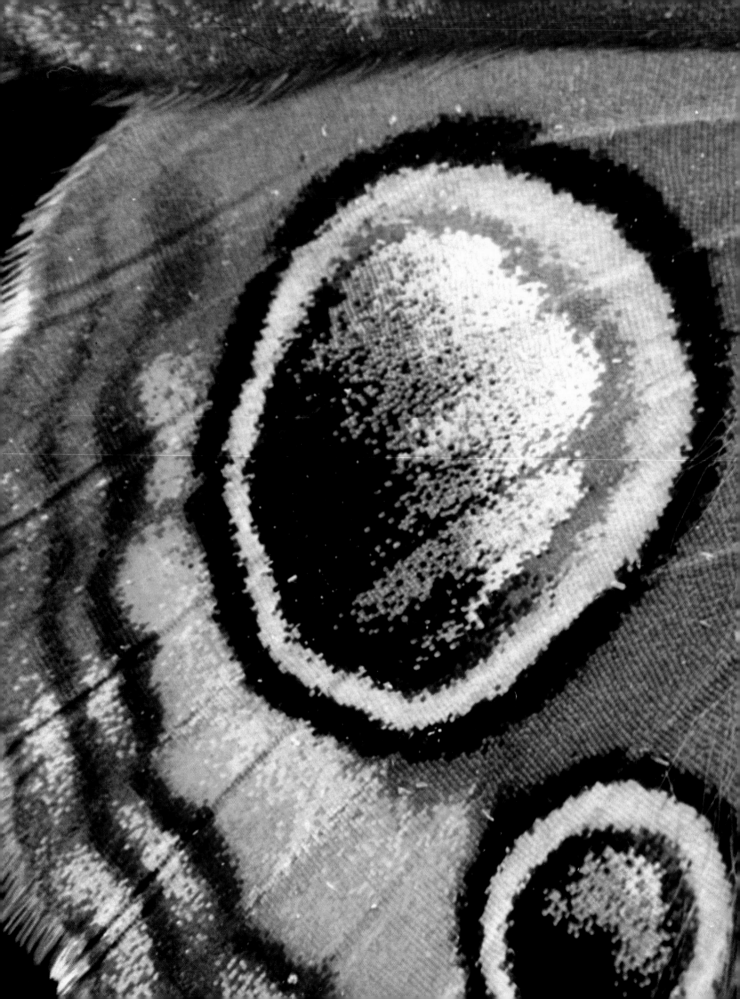

24

26

27

28

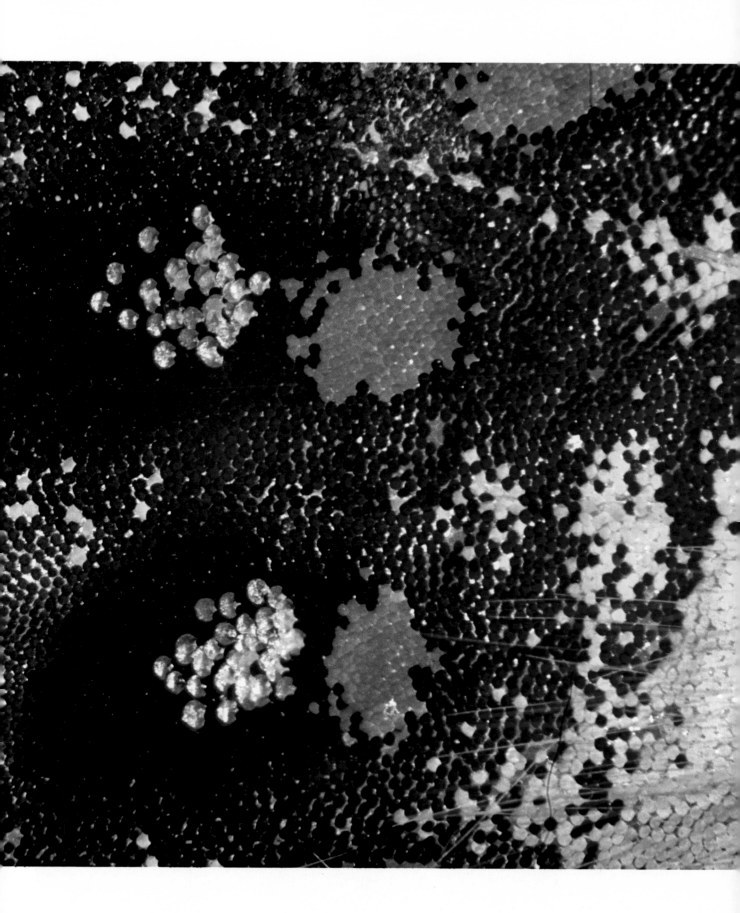

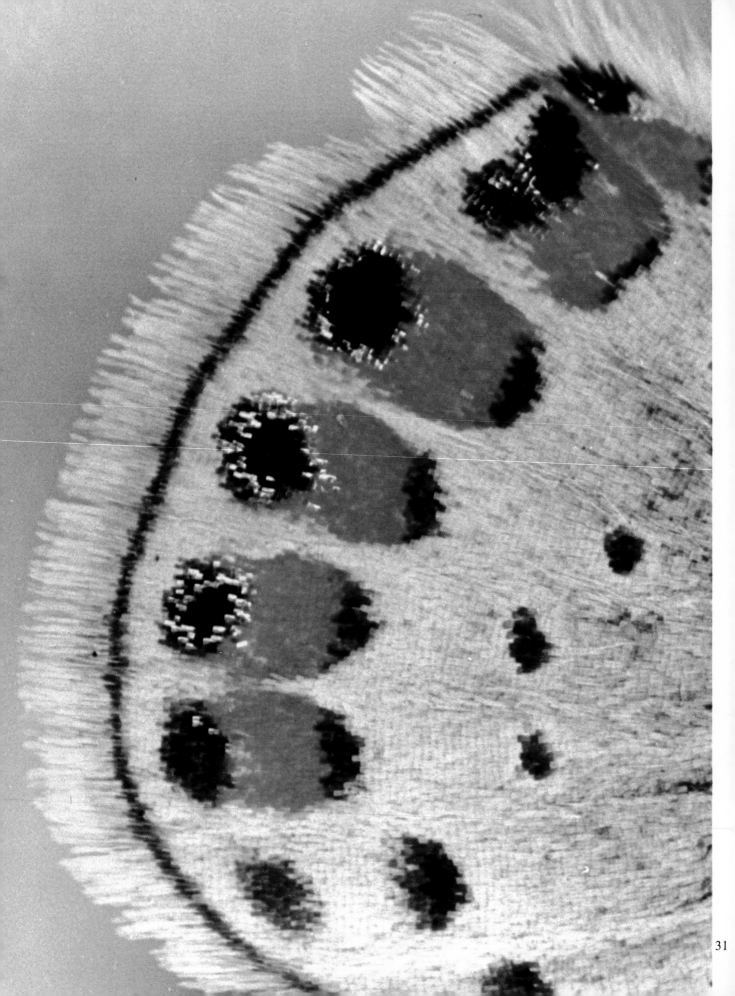

31

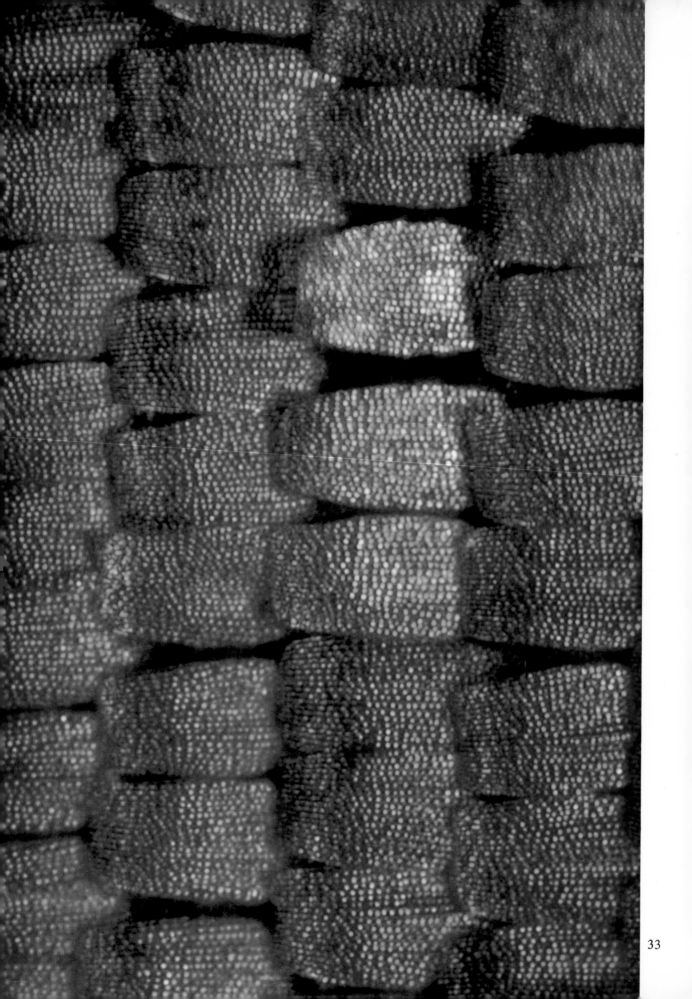

33

39

40

41

42

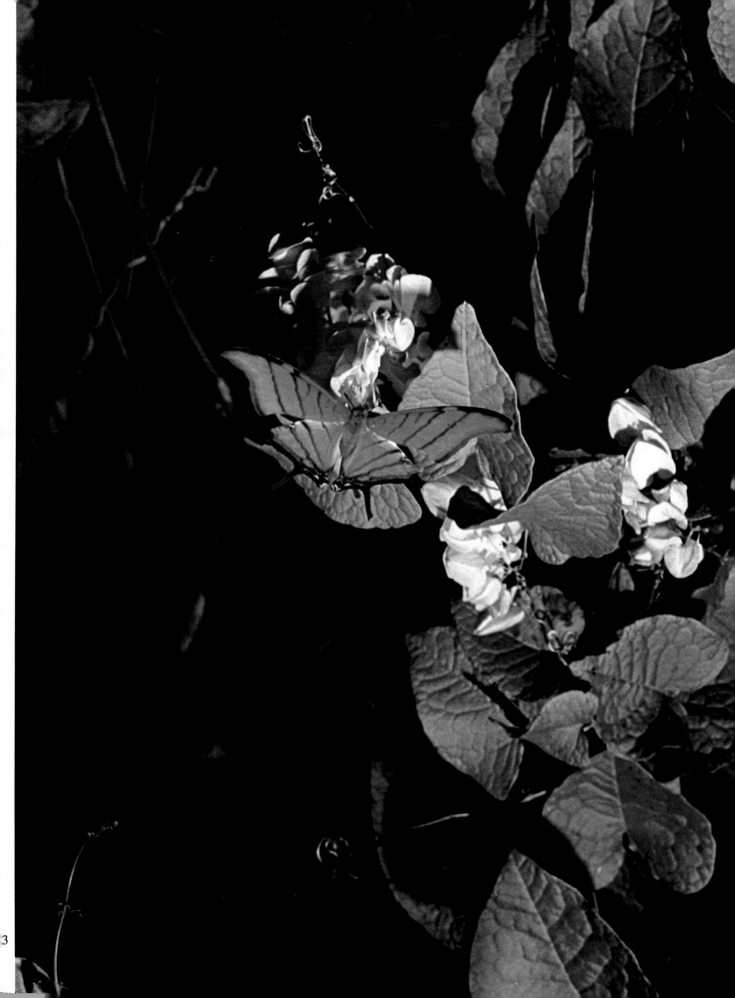

46

49

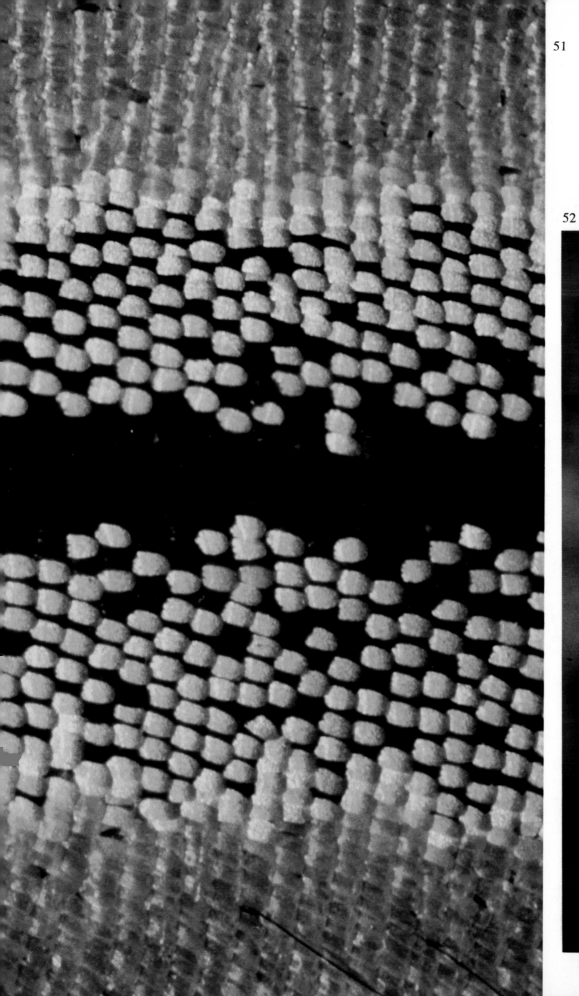

51

52

54

56

57

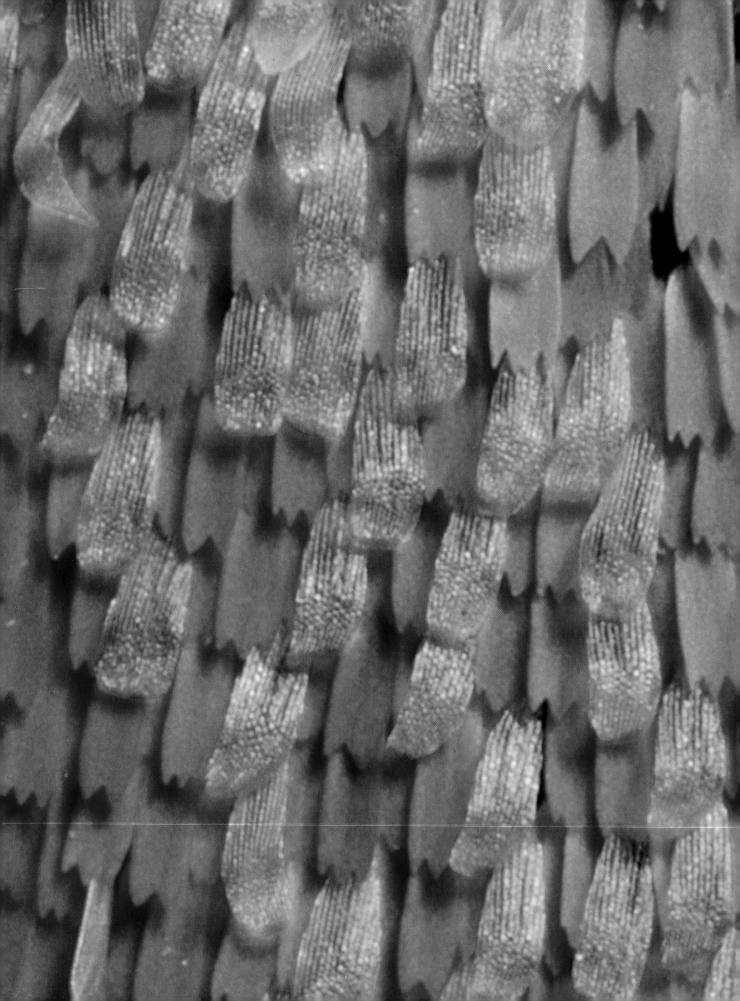

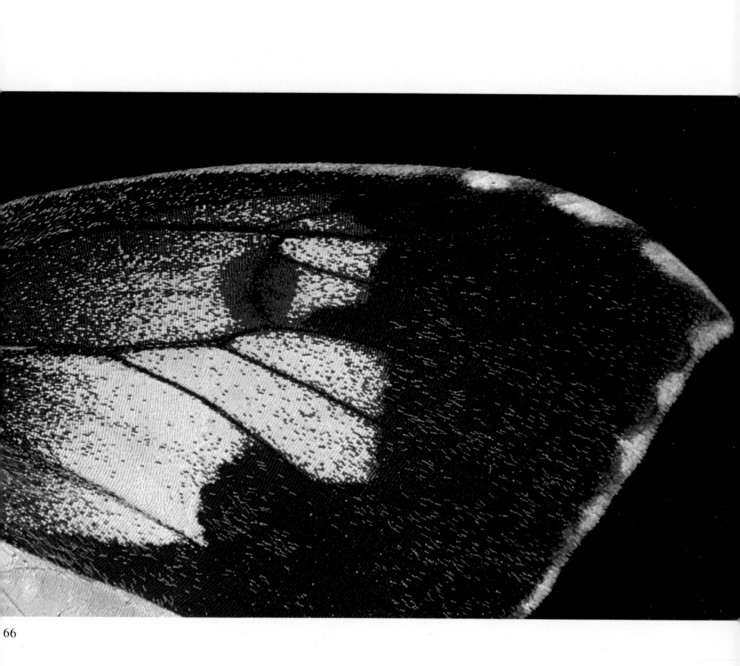

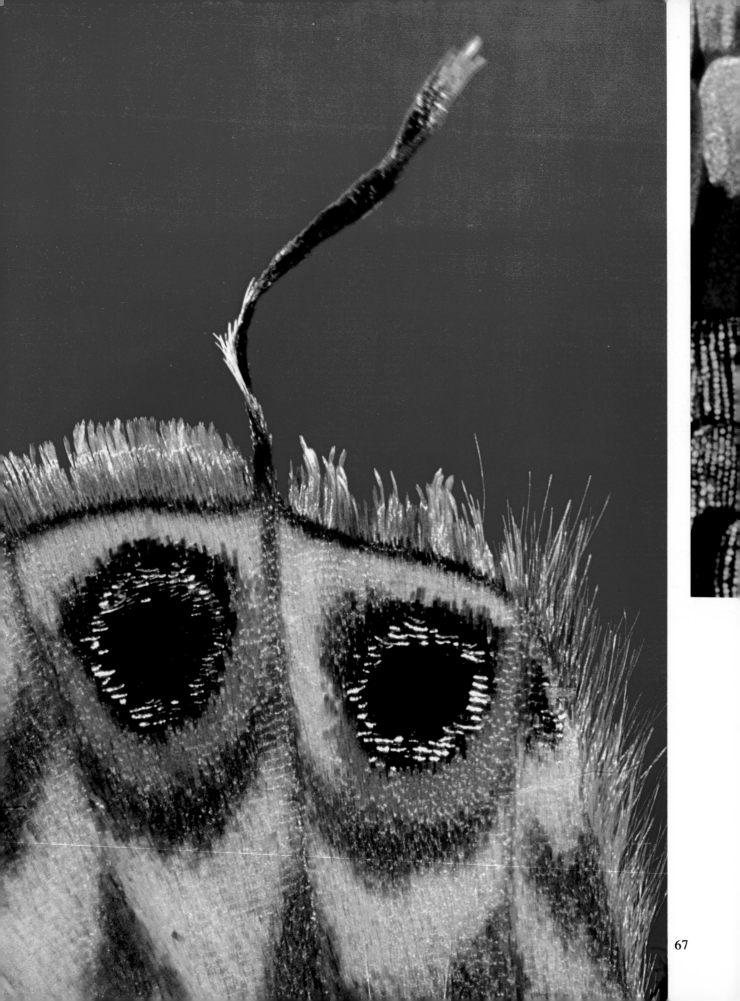

68

69

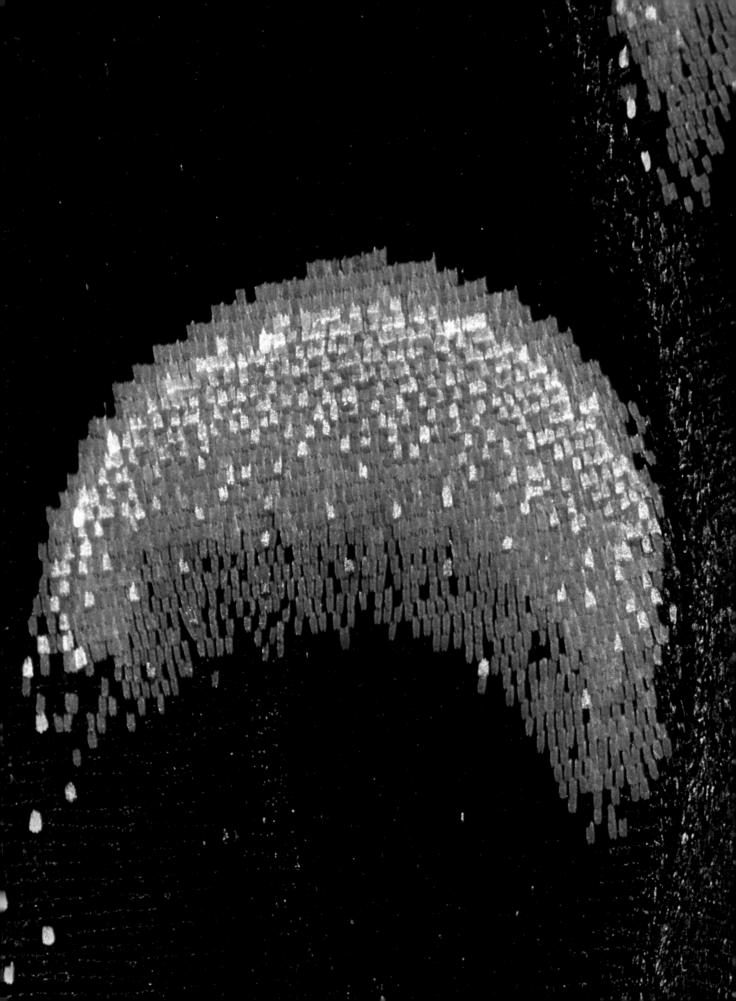

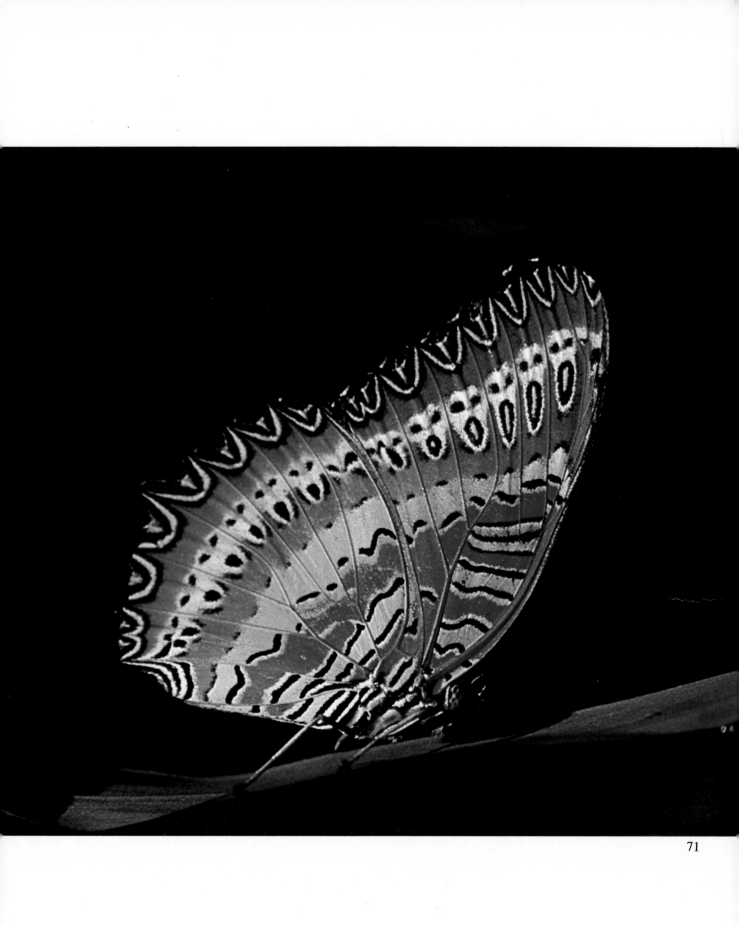

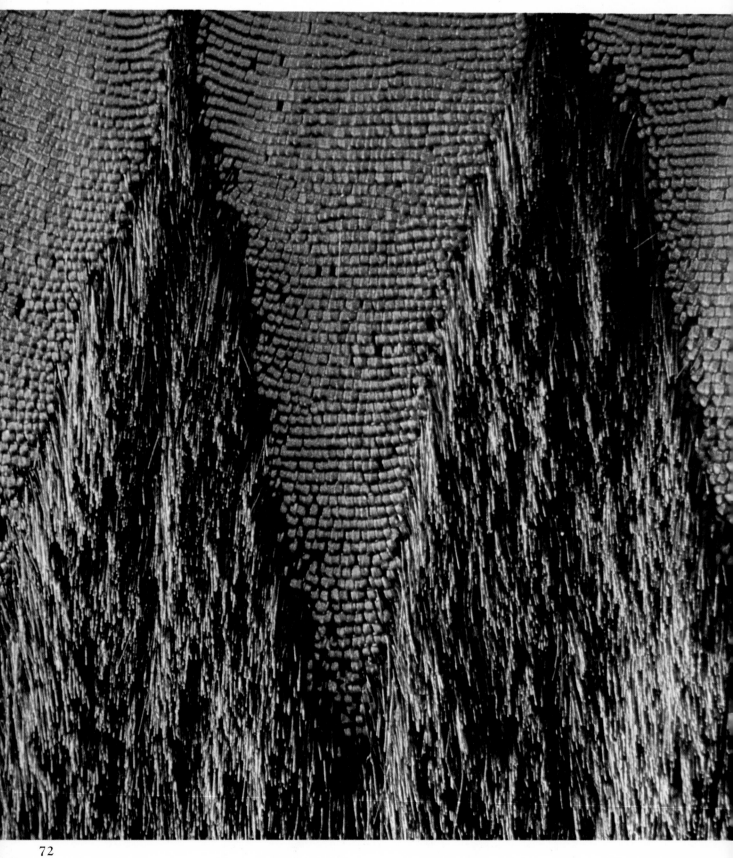

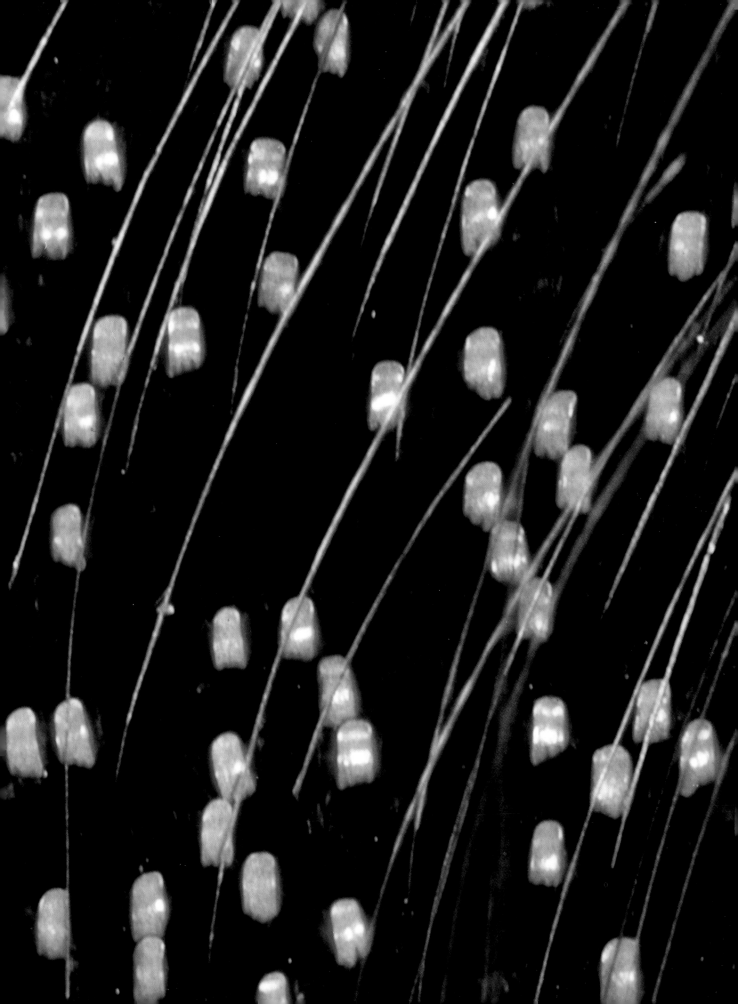

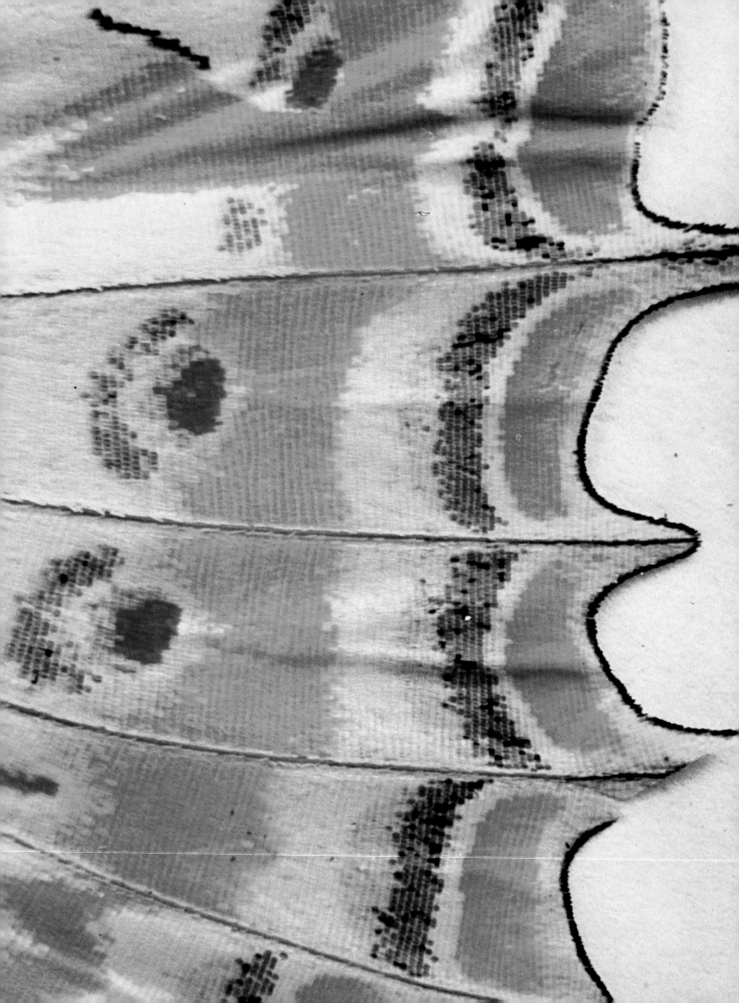

Notes to the Plates

Plate 1

One of the joys of living in the American tropics is watching the erratic sprints of Nemeobiidae such as this *Ancyluris aulestes* Cramer from Tingo Maria in Peru. The members of this family are all gaudily colored, and their iridescent flashes have prompted the common name Metalmarks.

Plate 2

One of the most spectacular sights of the South American forests is the flashing blue of the *Morpho*. Their jewel-like reflections can even be seen from low-flying aircraft hundreds of feet above the forest canopy. This feeding female *Morpho achillaena* Linnaeus from Amazonas, Brazil, would be easy to net if you were really stealthy. However, catching her in flight would be an entirely different matter. For survival the Morphos depend on their very fast, undulating flight and deceiving appearance. The flash of iridescent blue alternates with somber brown (see Plate 38), so as the insect rushes through the light and shade of the trees it is only intermittently visible and judging its distance becomes impossible. The best way to catch morphos is with a bait of overripe bananas mixed with stale beer. The bait should be set before dawn on an open path or glade where the insects are known to fly. Morphos are most active before noon, and about nine o'clock is the most likely time to find them. After imbibing the juices of the bait, the drunken insects can be picked up with the fingers. The addition of a piece of mirror or a dead morpho as a lure increases the effectiveness of the bait. However, it is comforting to know that the morphos used in the manufacture of jewelry are all insectary-reared, for perfect specimens are uncommon in the wild.

Plate 3

With folded wings the tails of *Marpesia petreus* Cramer touch the twig upon which it rests, and with the leaflike underside exposed, it evades the search of the inquisitive bird which saw it alight. Though this nymphalid is feeding on coral vine in Mexico, the species ranges from Kansas and Florida to South America. (See Plate 43.)

Plate 4

Known as the King Page or Giant Swallowtail, the papilionid *Papilio thoas* was first described by the Swedish doctor/naturalist Carl von Linné in the mid-eighteenth century. It is remarkable that so many of the common animals and plants we know today were first described and named by this remote and reclusive man more than two hundred years ago. Many of his original specimens are still preserved in the Linnaeus collection at the University of Uppsala in Sweden. Though he himself seldom traveled far, he received material from all over the world, and he is principally responsible for inventing the system of biological nomenclature we still use today. These particular butterflies are drinking from damp soil in Colombia.

Plate 5

This *Arawacus aetolus* Cramer from Amazonas, Brazil, is one of the most interesting bird deceivers known. The stripes focus the attention of the predator onto the least important end of the butterfly, where the wings are fashioned into a fake head complete with eyes and white-tipped antennae. The impression of the head is reinforced by the flaring of the lower edge of the wing membrane so that the "head" appears to have thickness, and the "antennae" are waved by rhythmic motions of the hindwings. A closely related and similar species of Lycaenidae has been observed to turn completely around upon landing, so the fake head occupies the expected position of the true one. This not only lessens the chance of serious injury if attacked, but enables the insect to take off in an unexpected direction if disturbed. One biologist has recorded that the butterfly walks backward to supplement the illusion, but it is much more likely that he too was deceived by the turnabout that the butterfly executes on landing.

Plate 6

The nymphalid *Siproeta stelenes* Linnaeus is widely distributed throughout Central and South America but is hard to catch for it flies high and fast over all but the tallest trees. It is a frequent but timid visitor to flowers, and its capture requires great patience and stealth. The pale color of the wing is produced by pigmentation of the wing membrane and almost total absence of scales. This specimen was photographed in Amazonas, Brazil. (See Plate 44.)

Plates 7 and 8

The two sides of *Anteos menippe* Huebner from Amazonas, Brazil, are very similar. In most tropical localities there are several species of *Anteos*-like butterflies which may be seen flying together and which to our eyes look almost indistinguishable. However, we now know that the wings of each sex and of each species have characteristic patterns of scales which reflect ultraviolet light. The butterflies, which can see ultraviolet light, therefore, have no difficulty in identifying their potential mates. In Europe the closely related *Gonepteryx* is among the first insects to herald the arrival of spring. Harry Clench has devised an intriguing but complex formula, involving the highest and lowest winter temperatures, by which one can predict the earliest spring day on which the first butterflies can be expected to emerge. These *Anteos* butterflies are lazy until disturbed, but their fast, uneven flight makes them very hard to catch.

Plate 9

A mating pair of *Melete lycimnia* Cramer from Venezuela. Sometimes a mating pair will take off and fly a considerable distance, the male (on the right) carrying the female as deadweight. Sometimes the female flutters as if trying to help, but as she faces backward it is doubtful that she does. Notice the deeper yellow markings on the sides of the body which may serve as positioning guides during courtship. This species is widely distributed over Central and South America.

Plate 10

Sometimes known as the Northern White Page, this resplendent papilionid *Eurytides protesilaus* Linnaeus is long-lived and a strong flier, so specimens as perfect as this one are most uncommon. This variable species occurs throughout Central and South America. Many American papilios feed on citrus and can become minor pests. Since they feed on nonpoisonous plants as caterpillars, we may presume the adults are palatable to birds and rely on speed and agility to avoid being eaten. Many specimens are known in museum collections with the impressions of bird's beaks upon their wings—they are the ones that got away! Experiments have shown that a butterfly with a damaged wing soon learns to compensate for the deficiency and is able to fly straight within an hour or so.

Plate 11

The prime function of veins in the wings of both butterflies and moths is to prevent undue flexing during flight. The thickened nature of the veins can be seen in this close-up of the wing of a ctenuchid moth. Not only butterflies are beautiful!

Plate 12

While the Nemeobiidae are adding color to South America, lycaenids like

Thysanotis regalis Smith and Kirby are brightening up New Guinea. The highly active and inquisitive disposition of these insects endears them to all collectors.

Plate 13

The underside of a small portion of the wing of *Ornithoptera priamus* Linnaeus shows the delicate way in which the pattern is constructed out of individually colored scales arranged like tiles on a roof. This wing is that of the yellow form *croesus* and comes from Batjan, in the Malay Archipelago. More information is given in the legend to Plate 51. Only the males are brightly colored and the dissimilar-looking dull-brown females were originally described as a separate species.

Plate 14

Varying from yellow to very pale green, the papilionid *Graphium tynderaeus* Fabricius from West Africa is a very strong flier and shares many features with the similar *Siproeta stelenes* (Plate 6) from South America. However, there can be no case for mimicry here for they are separated by the Atlantic Ocean, and few birds, if any, ever fly across to apply their previous experience.

Plate 15

Baeotus baeotus Doubleday and Hewitson, a brilliant butterfly with an almost white contrasting underside which makes it very difficult to follow in flight, and more particularly when it has landed and closed its wings. It is a frequent forest visitor to moist sand and fermenting fruit.

Plate 16

Contrary to popular opinion, not all moths are brown and dull-looking. This portion of wing is from the very beautiful and iridescent *Eucyane plagifera* Felder, a member of the Pericopidae.

Plate 17

The day-flying moth *Urania leilus* Linnaeus does not look unlike a papilionid butterfly. Though it is unusual for a large moth to be so gaudily colored, it is consistent with its daytime flight habits. The distribution of these flashy Urani-idae is at first sight curious, for they are known only from Central and South America (illustrated) and from Madagascar (see Plate 60). The explanation is that these are the only known locations of the food plant of their caterpillars. It is the distribution of *Omphalea* (Euphorbiaceae) that is curious, so the puzzle is passed to the botanists. In the Americas these moths regularly engage in massive migrations and can become so numerous that their corpses clog the radiators of automobiles.

Plate 18

The transparent ithomiids like *Greta andromica* Hewitson are delicate insects which are characteristic of the forests of Central and South America. Their wings are devoid of scales over most of the membrane so at rest they are all but invisible. These insects are unusual in that they obtain some of their nutrients from the juices of dead animals and bird excrement. They are not shy insects and if approached carefully can be picked up with the fingers.

Plate 19

The lycaenid *Callithea leprieuri* Feisth., seen resting on a wild orchid in Amazonas, Brazil, competes successfully with the nemeobiids (Plate 1) for brilliant iridescence. The metallic underside is complemented above with vivid indigo blue. One cannot but wonder if the red markings at the base of the wings are used in courtship. We do not know.

Plate 20

The color of the mother-of-pearl spots on the underside of the wings of *Danaida phrynichus* Fruhstorfer is achieved by the reflection of light from air-filled cavities in each scale. In this picture, taken in New Guinea, the brand on the hindwing can be seen as a dark mark. The brand is characteristic of male danaids, and during courtship the male inserts a brush of hairs, which are mounted on the posterior tip of the body, into a pocket on the upper surface of each hindwing in the region of the brand. One investigator alleges that a chemical reaction takes place between the secretions of the hairs and brand, generating an odor which stimulates the female into sexual excitement. If this is really so, it explains why so many other investigators have been unable to obtain reliable data on the function of each secretion on its own.

Plate 21

The tip of the hindwing of one of the few predominantly green butterflies, a male Kaiserihind *Teinopalpus imperalis* Hope, from southeast Asia. This insect is restricted to thick forests at altitudes between 6500 and 10,000 feet and has the reputation of being seen on the wing only before midmorning and rarely visiting flowers. Southeast Asia and the East Indies have more green butterflies than anywhere else in the world, but the reason for this is obscure.

Plate 22

Papilio iswara White from Malaysia has the mass of the wings broken up by a conspicuous white patch, but there is a second line of defense in the pair of "eyes" on each hindwing.

Plates 23 and 24

The Buckeye of the United States, *Junonia lavinia coenia* Huebner, tempts one to wonder what eyespots on the wings are really for. It has been shown experimentally by David Blest that the sudden presentation of eyespots startles birds more than the presentation of any other shape, so we presume this device gives the butterfly a moment in which to escape. The Buckeye has the reputation of being very pugnacious and capable of driving other butterflies away from his territory.

Plate 25

In Peru, as elsewhere in the tropical Americas, *Phoebis* butterflies assemble in large groups to imbibe moisture from drying puddles (they prefer soil moistened with cattle urine). Their sheer number affords them some protection, for if they are disturbed by a hungry bird, they arise as a swirling cloud, and the predator, unable to decide which one to pursue, tires before catching any of them. Notice how the butterflies are all aligned along the same axis. Unlike mammals and birds, butterflies can regulate their body temperature only by their behavior. When the air temperature is cool the butterflies orientate themselves at right angles to the rays of the sun so they expose the greatest surface area to the warmth. If they are already warm enough, they will face away from the sun so as to experience only the minimum heat gain. Blood in the veins of the wings distributes the heat throughout the body. Butterflies which emerge early in the year in temperate climates, and those occurring at higher altitudes, are usually darker than their fellows elsewhere. The darker color absorbs heat more readily so they are better adapted to cooler climates. Hence, midsummer broods of butterflies are frequently lighter than the spring and fall generations.

Plates 26 and 28

The jewel-like effects of the precise distribution of color are well displayed in these photographs of the scales of the hindwing of *Archon apollinus* Herbst from Syria and Asia Minor. However, one can see that a few scales are incorrectly colored, and it is variations such as these that allow overzealous collectors to convince themselves that they have discovered a new species.

Plate 27

The Dog Face or Dog Head, *Colias caesonia* Stoll, ranges from the northern United States through Central America to South America. The pattern on the wings of this specimen resembles the outline of a well-clipped poodle. The yellow pterine pigment in the wings of Pieridae, such as this example, is a waste product of the caterpillar which is stored and deposited in the wings as inert refuse.

Plate 29

These splendid little nymphalid butterflies with their elaborately designed hindwings seem to have real *joie de vivre* as they flit from perch to perch in the sunlight. This *Callicore sorana* Godart (underside illustrated here) occurs widely over southern South America. (See Plate 49.)

Plate 30

In contrast to the lower surface illustrated here, the upper side of this *Callicore eunomia* Hewitson is a brilliant metallic blue. The butterfly looks like a dazzling gemstone as it darts in and out of the shafts of sunlight penetrating to the forest floor. It always remains tantalizingly out of reach of a net.

Plate 31

The orange spots around the underside of the hindwings of *Plebejus emigdionis* Grinnell from California are subject to considerable variation, and ardent collectors greatly prize those with unusual arrangements. The wings of this species are fringed with unusually long hairlike scales.

Plate 32

Three male *Actinote demonica* Hopffmeister (Acreidae) in Peru are joined for a drink from wet mud by a *Yanguna pedaia* Hewitson (Hesperidae). Hesperids, commonly called Skippers because of their erratic bursts of flight, are rather mothlike in that they have large bodies and relatively small wings. Their close relationship to other butterflies is revealed by the swollen ends of the antennae, but they may be distinguished by the hooked tips. Skippers have especially good vision and are very difficult to catch once they are alerted. The acreids are among the most distasteful of all butterflies and are attacked only by inexperienced birds. Their poisonous properties are acquired from the members of the plant family Asclepiadaceae upon which their caterpillars feed. Notice the sucking tube or proboscis through which butterflies take in their food. It is clearly visible projecting from the lower part of the head of the Skipper in the middle of the picture. The kink in the middle of the proboscis is a constant feature.

Plate 33

Papilio ulysses Linnaeus is, perhaps, the most brilliant blue of all butterflies and gains its iridescence from the structure of each individual scale. The surface of each scale consists of laminations which are about one thousandth of a millimeter apart. Light of the longer wavelengths is trapped, so only the short wavelength blue escapes to be visible to the eye. The surface of the scale is coarsely ridged to enable the color to be seen from a wide range of angles. (See Plate 72.)

Plate 34

Morpho anaxibia Esp. from Rio de Janeiro is typical of the brilliance of male Morphidae, but it is unique in that the body is blue as well. The iridescent blue, which changes its hue as it is viewed from different angles, is produced by a series of ultrafine ridges along the length of each scale. There are between 1050 and 1400 ridges per millimeter, and the sides of each ridge are sculptured into layers of transparent parallel projecting platforms. The platforms are separated by a distance that ensures that all wavelengths of light are trapped except blue. As the wing scales are viewed from different angles, the effective distance between the platforms changes and so the color of the emergent light also changes. The surface of each scale is slightly curved so there is iridescence at all angles from which the wing is viewed. Under the surface sculpturing is a layer of black pigment, which ensures that all wavelength light is absorbed. This pigment eventually breaks down in old dead specimens. However, although the brilliance of the living insect does deteriorate to a small extent, the luster lasts indefinitely.

Plate 35

A large specimen of the papilionid *Troides miranda* Butler may measure seven inches across the wings and fully justify the common name Birdwing.

These magnificent insects are much prized by collectors. In order to ensure their survival they were included as protected species in the 1966 Fauna Protection Ordinance of Papua and New Guinea, but this covered only the National Parks. This particular specimen was photographed in New Guinea, but similar species occur throughout southeast Asia, the East Indies, the Philippine Islands and northeastern Australia. All the known forms feed on species of *Aristolochia* during the caterpillar stage and presumably store aristolochic acid as a toxin, which later protects the adults from birds.

Plate 36

Tasting experiments have shown that many papilionid butterflies, like this female *Parides anchises* Linnaeus from Venezuela, are extremely distasteful to birds and presumably other predators too. Lincoln and Jane Brower have used this species extensively in Trinidad for their studies on mimicry. Population studies have shown that the average life span of this butterfly is only from five to ten days, which is unusually short for a protected species.

Plate 37

The underside of *Morpho achillaena* Huebner from Rio de Janeiro, Brazil, is quite unlike the metallic blue upper side. It is this contrast in color that makes morphos so difficult to catch in flight. When alerted, they fly at about twenty miles an hour with a dipping motion. Some observers contend that males will deliberately taunt birds into chasing them, only to demonstrate that they cannot be caught. In this way naïve birds soon learn to leave them alone. The nondescript appearance of the underside provides excellent camouflage when at rest, and the small eyespots around the edge of the wing draw attention away from the more vulnerable parts of the body. However, the skeletal skin of the body is so tough that these insects have been seen withstanding being pecked by a bird.

Plate 38

The pastel shades of the underside of *Agrias narcissus* Staudinger from Brazil contrast dramatically with the strident blue and crimson of the upper surface. These high-flying butterflies are generally considered rare, but this only means that they are rarely seen. They can be baited with fermenting fruit, and this technique is responsible for the capture of most specimens.

Plate 39

One of the most widely distributed and common butterflies in the Americas is *Anartia amathea* Linnaeus, which may be found from southwestern United States to southern South America. When freshly emerged from the chrysalis, the male, illustrated here from Peru, has rich colors, but as the specimen ages the colors fade and the scales become worn. The female is pale and washed-out-looking from the time she emerges.

Plate 40

A mating pair of the delicate and tiny *Crocozona coecias* Hewitson from Tingo Maria, Peru. In Pieridae and Danaidae it is the male that most usually does the flying with the female being carried as a passive passenger, but in Lycaenidae, Satyridae, Hesperidae, and most Nymphalidae it is the female that is the active partner. The passive partner travels with the wings closed so the color pattern is concealed. In species of *Papilio* in which the female mimics distasteful models whereas the male does not, it is the female that exposes her colors by carrying the male. This role presumably confers some protection on the pair as they make their nuptial flight.

Plate 41

Details of one of the series of green flashes on the upper surface of the wing of a male *Trogonoptera brookiana* Wallace, the Rajah Brooke Birdwing from Borneo. (See Plate 69.) A real collector's item, these majestic butterflies can measure more than seven inches across the wings. Males gather gregariously in their jungle retreats and may sometimes be found in profusion drinking from mud moistened by urine, or even on fresh droppings. The females, which are larger but more somber, lead a solitary life, seeking out the food plant for their caterpillars. This species was described by Alfred Russel Wallace, an English naturalist who was a contemporary and friend of Charles Darwin. It was in fact Wallace who persuaded Darwin to publish their joint theory of evolution (with the help of ideas from Darwin's father) in 1859 under the title *The Origin of Species*. Had Wallace known how famous that book was to become he would surely have insisted on a joint authorship.

Plate 42

Looking porcelaneous and almost artificial, this female *Delias aruna* Boisduval from New Guinea is very conspicuous. The other species in this group have similar flamboyant underside markings but their upper sides are all uniform yellow or orange. This specialization of the under surface is unusual in butterflies and prompts one to wonder what is peculiar about their courtship. The uniformity of the upper surface may be deceptive, for it is possible that there are characteristic ultraviolet markings that we cannot see. However, that still does not explain the lower surface pattern.

Plate 43

Marpesia petreus Cramer feeding in Florida on a chain-of-hearts vine. The female illustrated here is paler than the male shown in Plate 3, but both are hard to see when they are at rest, due to the leaflike coloration of the underside of the wings. Experiments with other butterflies have shown that egg production can be raised threefold by making nectar available. Among the nectar-gathering insects like bees, butterflies, hoverflies (Syrphidae), and other flies, a hierarchy is established so there are no conflicts if two different insects arrive at a flower at the same time. One insect patiently awaits its turn while the other feeds.

Plate 44

This picture illustrates the underside of the butterfly *Siproeta stelenes* Linnaeus shown in Plate 6. As one would expect, the underside is much more somber in color.

Plate 45

Eurytides bellerophon Dalm. from Rio de Janeiro is one of the most spectacular papilionids in South America. Contrary to expectations based upon their conspicuous markings, these swallowtails are much sought after by birds and are seemingly good to eat. They rely principally upon their strong flight to escape capture.

Plate 46

This delicate little moth from Guatemala, *Cosmopteropsis thetysalis* Walker, is less than an inch across the wings but has a beauty to rival that of many butterflies.

Plate 47

Combinations of blue and brown scales produce beautiful patterns around the edge of the wing of *Chloreuptychia agatha* Butler from French Guiana. One can speculate whether the highlights are intended to simulate the light reflected from a dewdrop or from the lens of an eye.

Plate 48

Heliconius burneyi Huebner was probably among the complex of ninety-two red, black, and yellow butterflies encountered by Henry Bates on his voyage up the Amazon in the 1850s, and which first set him thinking about the phenomenon of mimicry. The members of the genus *Heliconius* are unusual among the butterflies in that in addition to imbibing nectar they also take pollen from the flowers they visit. The pollen is held on the tip of the proboscis by papillae and incubated with semi-digested nectar regurgitated from the crop (stomach). The liquefied pollen is then drawn into the crop and when further digested provides a substantial source of amino acids for protein building. This feeding technique may be at least partially responsible for the great longevity of *Heliconius*, for population studies have shown that both males and females may live up to three months in the wild.

Plate 49

The upper surface of *Callicore sorana* Godart contrasts sharply with the lower surface shown in Plate 29.

Plate 50

A common member of the mimicry complex in the Amazon Basin is this ithomiid, *Ceratinia tutia* Hewitson. In Trinidad, Brower and his co-workers collected many specimens by hanging bunches of dried heliotrope from the branches of trees. The butterflies visited the bait in great numbers, together with many other species of Ithomiidae and Heliconiidae.

Plate 51

Details of the structure of the scales of *Ornithoptera priamus* Linnaeus from Batjan. This species has a wingspan of six inches and occurs in three color forms: *urvillianus* is a brilliant blue and is found only on the Admiralty and Solomon islands; *poseidon* is metallic green and is widely distributed throughout the East Indies and northeastern Australia; and *croesus* (illustrated) is orange-yellow and is common in the Moluccas, Halmahera, Batjan, and other islands. The species is always difficult to capture as it flies high in dense forests. Professional collectors sometimes shoot these butterflies with dust shot. It is surprising that they are not severely damaged by this collecting technique. The females do not show these geographical variations and are all uniformly nondescript brown marked with grayish yellow. However, the females are probably the largest butterflies in the world, with wingspans of more than ten inches. These butterflies have the reputation of playing possum when disturbed in a situation in which flight is impossible. Some moths are renowned for this behavior, but with this possible exception it is unknown in butterflies.

Plate 52

The elegant *Papilio thoas* Linnaeus from Tingo Maria, Peru, is remarkably constant over its wide range from Mexico to southern Brazil.

Plate 53

The male *Parides tros* Fabricius illustrated here is rendered unpalatable to bird predators by poisonous compounds in the food plant of the caterpillar, which are carried through the chrysalis stage and stored in the adult body. This species is the model which is mimicked by the female of *Papilio torquatus*

116

Cramer. The male of *P. torquatus* is quite unlike the female, being black and yellow and with broader "tails" to the wings.

Plate 54

Strymon melinus Huebner, the Gray Hairstreak, from North Carolina is typical of many Lycaenidae in having a pair of false "antennae" developed from the hindwing margins, and centers of color where the head and eyes might be. These decoys attract the predator's attention away from the true head, so, if attacked, the insect may escape with only a tattered hindwing. This species is one of the relatively few butterflies which becomes a pest, as the caterpillars feed on beans and hops.

Plate 55

A transitional zone in the color pattern of *Papilio krischna* Moore from the Indian Himalayas. The difference in the structure of those scales that are metallic and iridescent and those that are colored solid red can be seen clearly in this photograph. The fine sculpturing responsible for the iridescence is too detailed to be seen at this magnification.

Plate 56

The wing outline is completely broken up by the fringing fingers in *Helicopis acis* Fabricius from Amazonas, Brazil. These butterflies can be abundant in swampy retreats where collectors rarely venture, and they are easily captured once located. This specimen is resting on a wild orchid.

Plate 57

Species of Satyridae, such as the *Euptychia mollina* Huebner illustrated here, have been used in mimicry experiments as the standard edible butterfly, for they are never refused by hungry birds or lizards. In palatability trials the experimental predator should eat a euptychid immediately after refusing the test insect; otherwise it could always be argued that the refusal occurred because the predator was not hungry.

Plate 58

In contrast to the euptychid in Plate 57, this ithomiid, *Oleria estella* Hewitson, is highly distasteful to birds. The transparency of the wings is achieved by the reduction of the scales to fine hairs, thus revealing the transparent membrane from which they are developed. In their preferred habitat of the shaded interior of the forest, these butterflies are very difficult to see on the wing or at rest. Therefore, the white patch presumably assists in species recognition. One would expect odor to play an important part in the courtship of these shade dwellers, for their vision must be severely limited by the lack of sunlight.

Plate 59

The nymphalid *Cyrestis acilia* Godart from New Guinea is superficially similar to species of the genus *Adelpha* in South America. Many butterflies have similar color patterns for no other reason than coincidence. There is a finite, though large, number of patterns that can be produced, and as the total number of existing species increases through evolution, it is inevitable that some will look alike.

Plate 60

The magnificent iridescent scales of *Chrysiridia madagascariensis* Less. belie the fact that this is a day-flying moth. In Madagascar this uranid is reared in insectaries to supply wings to the local jewelry industry and for export to manufacturers elsewhere in the world.

Plate 61

A copulating pair of *Mechanitis polymnia* Linnaeus, a highly distasteful member of the Ithomiidae which was a component of the mimicry complex discovered by Henry Bates during his voyage up the Amazon. The male (left) can be recognized by its straighter and more slender abdomen.

Plate 62

The silver spots on the underside of the hindwing of *Dione juno* Cramer are the visual equal of genuine mother-of-pearl, but are produced by the almost total reflection of light by air-filled scales. This specimen is drawing up liquid through its extended proboscis. Notice the elbow bend in the proboscis, which allows a long length of the end to be applied to the food.

Plate 63

In *Papilio krischna* Moore from Sikkim in northeast India, the red scales are pigmented and produce a solid color, whereas the lilac ones are weakly pigmented iridescent scales which produce their color mainly by optical effects. The difference in their gross structure can be seen in this photograph, which, as it was taken through a microscope, should properly be called a photomicrograph (a microphotograph is a photograph of microscopic size). (See also Plates 55, 68, and 70.)

Plate 64

Details of the scales of *Ornithoptera priamus poseidon* Doubleday, a Birdwing from New Guinea. Though the scales appear green and yellow, the differing hues are due only to the angle at which the scales are viewed. The scales themselves are transparent, the colors being produced by the optical effects of the microscopic architecture of the interior of each scale. (See also Plates 13, 51, and 73.)

Plates 65 and 66

The wing scales of *Colias eurydice* Boisduval are pigmented yellow, but the fine structure of the scales reflects only blue light when illuminated at certain low angles.

Plate 67

Fake heads are a common feature of the hindwings of Lycaenidae and are presumably effective in reducing their mortality at the beaks of birds. The antenna and eyespots shown here are of *Syntarucus pulchramurray* from Malawi.

Plate 68

Details of the scales of *Papilio krischna* Moore (refer also to Plates 55, 63, and 70). Experiments with descaled butterflies have shown that scales are not only decorative but are also aerodynamically important. The presence of scales increases lift by 15 per cent and improves the ability to glide.

Plate 69

This small portion of the compound eye of *Trogonoptera brookiana* Wallace (see Plate 41) shows some of the thousands of individual facets which draw light into each individual eye. Each eye probably forms a distinct image independently of its neighbors, so the butterfly sees its environment much as we would if we looked through drinking straws with blackened interior walls. Each single eye has a fixed focus lens, the outer convex surface of which can be seen in the photograph. The color pattern of the eye is an optical effect created by the pigment cells which isolate each eye from its neighbor. In living insects, particularly grasshoppers and tabanid flies, the color patterns seen in the eye are most spectacular and have even led some taxonomists to believe, momentarily, that they had discovered a new species.

Plate 70

Papilio krischna Moore has a row of orange-red crescents around the border of the iridescent green upper surface of each hindwing. The highlight of these semi-eyespots is produced by air-filled white scales. (See also Plates 55, 63, and 68.)

Plate 71

The scalloped edge of the wings of *Cethosia insularis* Felder from New Guinea is a characteristic feature of the members of this southeast Asian genus.

Plate 72

A portion of the forewing of a male *Papilio ulysses* Linnaeus (see Plate 33) from the Solomon Islands. The iridescent blue scales contrast markedly with the dense mat of highlighted black hairs. This is a high-flying jungle species which can, however, be attracted down to blue lures. These butterflies have a wingspan of up to five inches and are widely distributed throughout the rain forests of the East Indies and northern Australia.

Plate 73

A small area of the hindwing of *Ornithoptera priamus urvillianus* Guerin from the Solomon Islands. Here, toward the wing margin, the scales are giving way to hairs. (See also Plates 13, 51, and 64.)

Plate 74

The antennae of the male saturniid moth *Actias luna* are more plumose than those of the female (one of whose antennae is shown here), and can detect the scent of a virgin female from a considerable distance. In one experiment, marked males were released both eleven and four kilometers away from a captive female. Twenty-six per cent of the males discovered the female from the greater distance and 46 per cent from the lesser. This technique of attracting males with a captive virgin female is called "assembling" by moth collectors. It is successful only during that time of the day—usually late afternoon—when females normally emerge from the chrysalis. The absence of a club at the tip of the antenna is characteristic of moths.

Plate 75

The scent-disseminating hairs of a male *Prepona* (see Plate 15) are used to excite the female during courtship. The position of these hairs on the upper surface of the hindwing suggests that the male charges the tip of his body with scent from these hairs by elevating the abdomen and pressing it between the closed hindwings. The brilliant indigo of the major portion of the wing can be seen in the upper part of the photograph.

Plate 76

The hindwing margin of the *Polyura delphis* Doubleday from Siam shows an exquisite blend of color that would do justice to a summer print dress. This butterfly, which occurs throughout southeast Asia and the East Indies, is called the Jeweled Nawab. The leading edge of the forewing is unusual in having a serrated edge of unknown function.

Suggested Reading

AUSTRALIA

Common, I. F. B., and Waterhouse, D. F., *Butterflies of Australia.* Sydney and London: Angus and Robertson. 1972.

A compromise between a home and field book, with 498 pp., 26 color plates, 15 black-and-white plates, 25 figures, and 366 maps.

D'Abrera, B., *Butterflies of the Australian Region.* Melbourne: Landsdowne Press. 1971.

A general treatment of the butterflies, except the Skippers, of Australia, New Zealand and the nearby Pacific islands, such as Fiji and Solomon. 415 pp., 2362 color illustrations.

McCubbin, C., *Australian Butterflies.* Melbourne: Thomas Nelson. 1971.

A general treatment of the butterflies of Australia and Tasmania. 206 pp., 335 species illustrated in color from original paintings.

EUROPE

Higgins, L. G., and Riley, N. D., *A Field Guide to the Butterflies of Britain and Europe.* Boston: Houghton Mifflin. 1970.

A pocket field guide, 380 pp., 760 color illustrations.

JAMAICA

Brown, F. M., and Heineman, B., *Jamaica and Its Butterflies.* London: Classey. 1972.

A detailed treatment of the butterflies of Jamaica. 478 pp., 11 color plates.

TRINIDAD

Barcant, M., *The Butterflies of Trinidad and Tobago.* New York: Collins. 1970.

A general treatment of the butterflies of Trinidad and Tobago. 314 pp., 28 plates, some in color.

UNITED STATES OF AMERICA

Ehrlich, P. R., and Ehrlich, A. H., *How to Know the Butterflies.* Dubuque, Iowa: Brown. 1961.

A field guide to butterflies of North America north of Mexico.

262 pp., 525 black-and-white illustrations.

Klots, A. B., *A Field Guide to the Butterflies of North America East of the Great Plains.* Boston: Houghton Mifflin. 1951.

A pocket field guide, 349 pp., 247 color illustrations, 232 black-and-white photographs.

Mitchell, R. T., and Zim, H. S., *Butterflies and Moths. A Guide to the More Common American Species.* New York: Golden Press. 1964.

A pocket field guide, 160 pp., 423 color illustrations.

GENERAL BOOKS ON BUTTERFLIES

Dickens, M. C., and Storer, E., *The World of Butterflies.* New York: Macmillan. 1972.

Short notes on more than a hundred predominantly tropical butterflies. 127 pp., 108 color illustrations.

Gooden, R., *All Color Book of Butterflies.* London: Octopus Books. 1973.

A selection of world butterflies with extended captions. 72 pp., 101 color illustrations.

Lewis, H. L., *Butterflies of the World.* Chicago: Follett. 1973.

A pictorial identification to the butterflies of the world. 312 pp., 5885 species illustrated in color.

Riley, N. D., Werner, A., and Bijok, J., *Butterflies and Moths.* New York: The Viking Press. 1965.

A selection of annotated illustrations of butterflies and moths. 126 pp., 39 color plates.

GENERAL BOOKS THAT INCLUDE BUTTERFLIES

Klots, A. B., and Klots, E. B., *Living Insects of the World.* London: Hamish Hamilton. 1959.

A general account of the insects. 309 pp., 125 black-and-white and 152 color photographs.

Linsenmaier, W., *Insects of the World.* New York: McGraw-Hill. 1972.

A comprehensive natural history of insects. 392 pp., 160 color plates.

Stanek, V. J., *The Pictorial Encyclopedia of Insects.* London, New York, Sydney, Toronto: Hamlyn. 1970.

A general account of the insects. 544 pp., 960 black-and-white and 77 color illustrations.

Wickler, W., *Mimicry in Plants and Animals.* New York: World University Library, McGraw-Hill. 1968.

An excellent paperback on mimicry. 249 pp., 22 black-and-white and 31 color illustrations.

Wigglesworth, V. B., *The Life of Insects.* Cleveland and New York: World Publishing. 1964.

A general account of the insects. 360 pp., 24 black-and-white and 12 color plates, 164 line illustrations.

Index

(Numbers in italics are plate numbers.)